The Angel of Absolute Zero

The Poiema Poetry Series

Poems are windows into worlds; windows into beauty, goodness, and truth; windows into understandings that won't twist themselves into tidy dogmatic statements; windows into experiences. We can do more than merely peer into such windows; with a little effort we can fling open the casements, and leap over the sills into the heart of these worlds. We are also led into familiar places of hurt, confusion, and disappointment, but we arrive in the poet's company. Poetry is a partnership between poet and reader, seeking together to gain something of value—to get at something important.

Ephesians 2:10 says, "We are God's workmanship . . ." *poiema* in Greek— the thing that has been made, the masterpiece, the poem. The Poiema Poetry Series presents the work of gifted poets who take Christian faith seriously, and demonstrate in whose image we have been made through their creativity and craftsmanship.

These poets are recent participants in the ancient tradition of David, Asaph, Isaiah, and John the Revelator. The thread can be followed through the centuries—through the diverse poetic visions of Dante, Bernard of Clairvaux, Donne, Herbert, Milton, Hopkins, Eliot, R. S. Thomas, and Denise Levertov—down to the poet whose work is in your hand. With the selection of this volume you are entering this enduring tradition, and as a reader contributing to it.

—D.S. Martin
  Series Editor

The Angel of Absolute Zero

POEMS BY
Marjorie Stelmach

CASCADE *Books* · Eugene, Oregon

THE ANGEL OF ABSOLUTE ZERO

Cascade Books
An Imprint of Wipf and Stock Publishers
199 W. 8th Ave., Suite 3
Eugene, OR 97401

www.wipfandstock.com

PAPERBACK ISBN: 978-1-6667-3812-4
HARDCOVER ISBN: 978-1-6667-9843-2
EBOOK ISBN: 978-1-6667-9844-9

Cataloguing-in-Publication data:

Names: Stelmach, Marjorie
Title: The Angel of Absolute Zero / Marjorie Stelmach
Description: Eugene, OR: Cascade Books, 2022 | Poiema Poetry Series.
Identifiers: ISBN 978-1-6667-3812-4 (paperback) | ISBN 978-1-6667-9843-2 (hardcover) | ISBN 978-1-6667-9844-9 (ebook)
Subjects: LCSH: 1. American poetry—21st century. I. Religion and poetry. II. Series.
Classification: CALL NUMBER 2016 (print) | CALL NUMBER (ebook)

FEBRUARY 28, 2022 10:36 AM

for Dan

Contents

The Divestments of Autumn

How It Is We Have Come to This

The Late Accommodations

Tenebrae

Churches are best for prayer that have the least light.
—JOHN DONNE

It looks the same.
Shadowy crosses tremble in the long aisle.

Saints recede into darkened archways.
The organ softly takes up being lost—a minor key,
                        somber, remote.

In candlelit pews, soft garments shift their folds,
aligning with the murmur of prayer.

Down all these years it returns, the order of service.
I follow to the end
                and leave in silence.

I wasn't looking for a way back,
only to close the day against an old error.
                        A day as long as ever.
An error even longer.

Canticle of Want

Canticle of Want

Let me not be blamed for the script, for the ink is bad
and the vellum defective, and the day is dark.
—ANONYMOUS SCRIBE

Lord of stone cliffs and the guileless trill
       of the canyon wren, of stunted hemlocks,

imperiled coasts; Lord of the fragile nitrogen cycle,
       vanishing aquifers, spreading deserts;

Lord of neglect and carelessness, of greed
       and depletion, the doleful call of the loon;

Lord of ruin, of remnant and ragtag, of making do,
       you too must want as fiercely as we do,

your world being almost nothing but want.

Each year in the heartland, twilight breezes
       slide easily over our furrowed acres

sowing all manner of wanton seeds;
       a red-shouldered hawk wheels and watches;

its shadow wheels and is watched. Each harvest,
       a full moon, drastically magnified, rises—

a trick of the eye no one can account for: so much
       is beyond our knowledge. For more than

two hundred thousand years, our kind has studied
       this earth; we have yet to discern your purpose.

How badly we want to believe in your good intentions.

For centuries, monks dipped quills into inks
        concocted from hawthorn, salts, and wine.

They lived in vigilance, hidden away, recording
        your hints and evasions; they died

of their times, as we do. We're told they stayed faithful.
        It's harder now. Today, no one doubts

who owns the heavens: American drones cross
        invisibly over invisible borders; refugees

trudge toward rumors of air drops. Brevity haunts us.
        Every moonrise augurs departure. By night,

we children of plenty labor over our keyboards,
        documenting our days in a digital light

we have found no way to erase. How badly we want
        to escape all notice, want equally not to be

lost sight of. Lord, whose name is Everlasting,
        how could we think you would understand?

The Lost Blue of Chartres

By the 12th century, the deep cobalt blue
in the stained glass of Chartres was a secret lost.

The blue was born
in an age of faith,
an age of filth.

Some say it derived
from peasant sweat,
from smears

of soot, from piles
of excrement underfoot,
or the muck tramped back

to the worksite from huts
shared with beasts.
Some scholars believe

its source was potash
leached in iron pots
to a white salt. Others,

inclined to the abstract,
claim
it clung like mold

to the architects' scrolls—
a fur of hubris,
delusion, corruption.

Mystics will tell you
the blue was never *born*:
it was simply there—

in the water, in the air,
in the soil.
Art historians insist

that a blue fog hung
in that century's lanes—
a breath exhaled

from birch tree forests.
Folktales swear
the blue was pressed

into the villagers'
very skin,
that it darkened

their life-lines,
the creases of their faces,
the backs of their knees.

Or maybe it arose
in diaphanous coils
from votive candles

to hover, cold,
in the half-built hulk.
But everyone agrees

it's gone.
Like so much else.
Like souls.

Those who long for the blue
even now
must turn to prayer:

Lord of our benightedness,
give us this day
our impure world

to make of it
what bread we can.
What legends of our own.

What stains. What light.

Unjust

Finding no traction on the slippery slant
of greenhouse glass,
a ragged gang of robins plunks
their little butts in the guttered snow
to drink from the metal trough where,
                    just

below their nodding beaks, a sheet
of mirrored clouds floats, and underneath,
it's springtime: tended rows of tender green.
Now and forever. World without end.
But not for the robin flock. For them, it's
                    just

a world *without*—a plight they're long
familiar with. At intervals, a stubborn
or unworldly one is lured again to light
on the glass, but the slope remains too steep
for grip, the sky un-giving, and in the end it's
                    just

another promised land not meant for them.

The Psalm of the Luna Moth

After a Luna moth egg hatches, the caterpillar moves
through five instars, eating constantly, then weaves
a cocoon from which it emerges mouthless. As an adult,
it flies only at night, and lives only long enough to mate—
a few days at most.

Those innumerable feet
seemed so useful
in my youth,

but looking back, I see
it was a life spent crawling,
chewing.

Then, you called me.

     Here am I.

You freed me, first, from hunger
and the sorrow of my plodding,
and now,

in fields of luminous dusk,
beneath a silken beckoning
of stars,

you have given me wings
and coupled my heart
to the moon.

Lord of Light, I have felt
my wings beset
by the forces

of your suddenness,
your swerves and lifts, your
sheer drops.

And now,
having come into the fullness
of my longing, once again

I hear your voice.

> *Here am I.*

Eagerly, I spread my wings
and all my previous lives
before you

to ask what you,
in the sweep of your reckless love,
will make of me next.

The Laws of Perspective

*Every painting comes from far away (many fail to
reach us), yet we only receive a painting fully if we
are looking in the direction from which it has come.*
—JOHN BERGER, RE: FRA ANGELICO

In those days, the stricken
were brought on stretchers to a place

where the overland roads of the Empire
met, intersected, ran on.

There the afflicted were lowered to the shoulder,
eased as they could be, kissed, if they could be,

and left in the hope that a healer might come
from afar who would not look away.

The painting, too, has come from afar,
a girlchild visited by an angel, both figures

bowed to the arc of a narrative so time-worn
you'd swear you knew it in the womb.

Two perfected gestures, met on the wooden panel—
the virgin's crossed arms, the angel's bent knee—

transfixed in gold light,
in the instant before it will be too late.

When Fra Angelico's miracle finds you,
the age of faith will be well in your past.

You'll be at your own crossroads peering,
as warned, in the wrong direction. Even so,

the moment will shimmer. Your gaze will be fixed
on the virgin / the angel / the receding archways

of a century unschooled in the laws of perspective,
a world still blinking at the two-dimensional.

Of course, yours is a modern vision—
a shrewd eye, a single cocked eyebrow. Still,

you'll recognize this as a crossroads. You'll lean in,
as if to stop the disaster—a young girl crushed

by the wheels of acquiescence. Or you'll watch,
amazed, as the oils thicken and suddenly,

piercingly, there are three: a girlchild,
a messenger angel, a Child.

Or none of the above. You'll stand there,
stricken, on the brink of your age and its failure

to save you. You, cradled in your own crossed arms
in the arched entryway of a cold museum gallery

while, from afar, they come bearing down upon you,
four unfurled dimensions come to crush you.

Come to crush us all. And this is the moment
foretold: you look away.

In the Cave

The cut off for human compassion currently falls
"somewhere between a shrimp and an oyster."
—PETER SINGER

i.
Oh, Heart, here we are again in the cave

decanting a litany of beasts that dwell
       in peripheral vision with ill intent:

the furtive urban rat, the spider
       in a dust-grimed corner crouched

above her white ball of children,
       the pent constrictor coiled to strike.

In atavistic dreams, I hear the click
       of spurs on rock—bats emerging

in legions to steer my shadowed lawn,
       tangle my hair, drink my blood.

ii.
Deep December. A little brown Missouri bat

masked in a foul white pastiness awakens
       in fever, packed shoulder to shoulder

with thousands of kin, wakes to the yeasty
       smell of contagion. Restlessness wrinkles

the living walls, where bats, letting go of their place
       in the mass, drop to the cave floor, stricken.

]

For the little brown bat, the world's amiss:
        a stickiness blots its facial fur, each breath

comes damp and clotted. Thirst sends it out
        into blinding daylight and frigid cold, where

it struggles to fly, but its wing tissues, strangely
        tacky and matted, adhere at the folds.

Lurching in crooked circles, it hurls itself
        repeatedly upward until it collapses—

a dense lump of fur on frozen ground,
        as though an owl had found it, had

dropped it—scabrous, eyes crusted,
        nose white with frost.

Not frost. Fungus.

iii.
I stumble upon it—exhausted, still prying

its rent wings open. One dying bat
        among many, strewn down the slope

to the lake, convulsing, eyes clenched against
        shattering sunlight, a demonic snarl

twisting its rat face: *a dreadful creature*!
        Then, I lean closer: *a dreadful death*!

It's only now I remember: a bat plague
        is sweeping the country—

white-nose syndrome. And I think, *cocaine.*
        I begin—I can't help it—creating for him

a death rush come riding the thin winter sun,
        photons cascading through rods evolved

for the dimness of starlight, arriving to dazzle
        his dying vision, his heart rate speeding

toward no-space-at-all-between-beats, a flat line
        of rapture. Poor little creature,

innocent victim of a vile fungus, a loathsome,
        skin-sucking, many-mouthed demon

beyond comprehension, beyond all redemption:
        pure living evil!

Oh, Heart, here we are again in the cave.

Tremolo

It's less often now that a late spring dusk
tenders over the darkening waters a loon's otherworldly call.

Sixty million years of loon song brought to perfection.
To which my heart answers *lorn*, answers *yore*,

answers *ruth, erstwhile, thole*—long-drawn vowels
in a language more and more bereft of meaning.

◆

The loon alone among birds has evolved solid bones,
an achievement both boon and affliction—

the ease of the long dive bought at the cost
of swiftness in lift-off—a perilous bargain.

Some nights, their tremolos hold only loss, rising
over our glacial lake to rinse and shiver my marrow

with word of a day when our voices, too, will haunt
a planet we no longer walk, our cries rising ghostly

from silvery disks left to spin for a time in our wake,
filling the night with saxophones, cellos, violas.

◆

That all calling is calling to an Other who has never
answered—this is the Sorrow itself, a honing

of the heart, only complete when our capacity
for grief has evolved to meet our capacity for longing.

Tonight, it seems likely to come in my lifetime—
our lake's last loon call. One more hurt in time's

long harrowing, a cry from the dark
to which our language will own no answer.

Lack

Out in the easement,
windfall limbs build haphazard trellises nothing climbs.
Not enough nails in the wind to repair
             the ramshackle of it.

A woodpecker turns
his skilled attention from the bark of a persimmon
to the last of its bitter fruit. One taste and he's off
                 into vacuous sky.

High overhead,
a lone hawk circles: nothing here to see. Any creature
hunkered here past solstice has made, like me, a choice:
                        abstinence; austerity.

Listen: only scoffing calls
from a flock of blackbirds steeped in lack, asking nothing,
expecting less. At dusk, they vanish into their beaks.
                  After dark, I can only imagine.

The Angel of Absolute Zero

There will be nine billion of us
on the planet by mid-century.

Because no atom of the angel stirs, we hang
       her image above our babies' cribs,
in the hope that our young will aspire
       to her purity, learn to live on less:

first, a Sabbath fast, then holy days
       of foodlessness, until they feed on
nothing as often as they can. As soon
       as they can talk, we teach them

to pray: *Forgive us our breath, as we*
       forgive those who are born
among us. Older, they learn the one
       beatitude: *Blessed are those who*

hunger and thirst after righteousness
       alone. At school they'll read
the *Parable of the Sower,* a tale in which
       seeds return from the dead.

When it rains, when it rains . . . , we sing
       into their dreams, praying
they might last that long. Lying in the dark
       apart from each other, we invoke

the immaculate heart of the angel,
       praying for the strength
to explain to our children why they, too,
       do not deserve to live.

Toxic Nocturne

Early Onset with Quicksand and Pythons

On one of our walks last winter,
    you warned me about the pythons.
Joking, I thought. But as weeks passed,
    pythons kept coming up. By summer,
your pace had slowed. Names evaded you,
    students mostly. Then, colleagues.
Soon, your sentences faltered. You shuffled.
    One day, you halted abruptly, alarmed
at a crack in the sidewalk, certain we'd come
    to the edge of a drop-off.

Pythons turned up in the headlines that fall,
    Burmese invaders of record-breaking lengths,
spreading alarmingly through the Everglades.
    But you had a plan. With grizzlies or elk,
the rule, you explained, was *get big*:
    fill your lungs to capacity, spread
your elbows, hulk. You were pretty sure
    it would work on pythons.

All winter in the care center, pythons
    invaded your dreams. You confessed
you were frightened for your daughters:
    how could they ever *get big* enough
to survive? Your fears took me back
    to a story I'd heard—a eulogy really,
at my brother's memorial service.
    His best friend from childhood told how,
as kids, they'd sit around Saturday mornings
    arguing over the most ridiculous stuff,

like: What if you fell in a pool of quicksand?
    Is it better to struggle to reach for a branch

on the edge, or to spread yourself flat and wait
        to be rescued? The quarrels morphed into
contests: whose breath would be first to give out
        when both of them sank completely
beneath the surface? My brother, he finished,
        nearly sobbing, had let him win.

I've read that, these days, bounty hunters
        patrol the Everglades searching for pythons.
I wish I could tell you how right you'd been
        to prepare us, could thank you, could
reassure you your daughters have grown
        big enough to scare off the common monsters.
As for the rest of us, we're all still here, holding
        our breath as we wait to be rescued.

When I think of you now, I think of whales,
        another true story, how they started
in the seas like the rest of us, then moved
        onto land where they ruled the earth
for millions of years. They were really big,
        the largest predator ever, so mostly
they died of natural causes. But then,
        for no reason anyone knows, they turned
and walked back into the sea.

Whales swam off Florida's Gulf Coast back
        when the state was mostly submerged.
They swim there today—endangered now.
        Thirty million years of evolution,
and they haven't yet learned to breathe underwater.
        I wonder if they've had second thoughts.
If asked, I'd advise them to stay in the ocean.
        Life grows more perilous daily on earth—
quicksand everywhere, all these pythons.

First Sighting of the Great Salt Flats

The mountains opened with a classic gambit: duplicity.
Shimmering in the dawn light, they seemed nearby—

a day's walk, a day and a half. Glinting from their slopes
ran the sweet, cold waters the travelers had tasted

in their dreams for weeks. Nothing in this journey
had been easy—maps undependable, wagons

teetering on collapse, the river when they reached it,
in flood, the ford erased. Trees stood fifty yards

from shore, their branches slapped by a mean current
rushing with corpses of small furred creatures. Deer, too,

and living snakes. They'd waited long days
on the river bank under a ceaseless wheel of buzzards

while, on the flood's far side, the season turned
against them.

To spare the oxen, they began to prune
the wagons' excess weight, the only move open.

They unloaded bedsteads, mirrors, the heirloom dishes,
stuffed the contents of heavy trunks into pillow slips.

They couldn't do without the saws and axes,
the grinding stone, spinning wheel, butter churn.

The family Bible was too dear to lose. The fiddle.
The cradle. As for the rest? They placed

their belongings at the side of the trail
and watched as they grew smaller.

Then came a second pruning much like the first.
They left the bodies one by one—deaths from exhaustion,

hunger, despair. Their tongues ran out of words to speak
above the graves. Tears were kept to the privacy of wagons.

Remote, the mountains watched the board. They never
made a second move: the game was always theirs.

Farther west than anyone knew, California offered
no hope. Already it had its own bones to bury.

And so, they trekked from one grave to the next.
The few who straggled, half alive, through what was surely

the last of the passes, looked out over a wide white glitter,
sank to their knees and wept for joy:

the dazzle ahead—it could only be sunlight
sparkling on the water.

Precious Oils

Larry at the gas station shocks me this morning
>with a naked head, his silky curls shorn.

He grins as I fill my tank with pricey unleaded.
>His head, it turns out, is surpassingly fine,

and, ah, how the morning light loves it. As the numbers
>run, I envision an intimate scene between us:

long strokes of the shears, a soft fall of curls,
>and the buzz of the razor as it bares

bright swathes of Larry's scalp arced above
>the cerebral folds of Larry's *Self*.

I love how baby brains arrive as smooth as Larry's
>pate, then pleat and furrow into *us*,

love too how language whispers its half-rhymes
>into my consciousness: *storage* and *knowledge*—

hints of a buried kinship. Take *gasoline:* dactylic?
>anapestic? A serious trochee across the pond:

petrol still clinging to the old rock. Meanwhile,
>in a nearby bog, the slow burn of flesh goes on:

ancient, leathered faces as bewildered as our own.
>*O, fossil child of silence and slow time . . .*

In an age lit by a softer light, whalers tracked
>their stately prey, avid to render

its grey bulk down to gold. Meanwhile, above
        the grisly work, a string of whale-oil lamps

pendulum'd over the slickened decks. *Cranium*
        and *pendulum*, another fertile rhyme,

cross-breeding human knowledge and the steady
        swing of cold steel. I want to rhyme

progress and *precious*—a stretch. *Progress* and
        unease? Worse. *Precious* and *perilous*?

Today, in Northern seas, another damaged
        freighter spreads its oils on the waters.

The cost in wings, the cost in eggs, the cost
        in song. Below, peering from crenellated

sockets, whales with brains as lit as my own
        are forced to navigate dark waters

our age has rendered *perilous*. Standing at the pump,
        I steer a path through moral reefs,

rhyming *oil* and *subliminal*, tasting complicity.
        But Larry is waiting for payment.

The total seems excessive. Regardless, I'll pay.
        In the greater scheme, it costs me little.

Time will ease my guilt and soon, speaking
        geologically, will erase all traces

of our kind—these *Selves* that have cost the earth
        so much more than we intended.

Toxic Nocturne

       Toxic, undrinkable—
hard not to think it,
       gazing out over
the oil-slick waters
       stretching below
this glass-walled room
       where I've come alone
to slake my grief
       with wine and watch
the lake's gray deepen.
       Instead, I'm pounding
the window glass,
       trying to startle
a shadow-draped deer
       stilled at the shoreline
too far to hear me.
       A doe.
Cautious creature,
       why doesn't she know
not to sip—not from this
       or from any dark cup
too impure to reflect
       her grave composure?
Turning, as if she were
       gauging a danger,
she pauses for one
       long moment before
bending again
       to the pewter gleam,
and I've no way to stop her.
       She breaks through
the shimmer, parting
       the waters to quench,
at what cost, her
       (yes, I know: *terrible*)
terrible thirst.

We Walk Invisible

We have the receipt of fern-seed, we walk invisible.
—HENRY IV, PART 1
ACT II, SCENE I

Instinct

Among the sweepings of another winter, I find
on the screened porch a lump of grayish fur
and, wedged in a corner,
            a single scalloped wing.
How many days did this bat live
to hurl its flesh against the wire grid?
How many times knocked back
                        to the floorboards,
each flight a greater damage,
sonar out of true and nothing else to try
until the final spiraling climb
            on the one remaining wing?
The last task's mine:
to sweep these soft remains down the cabin steps
and into the lattice of ferns at the forest's edge.

Magic

Act ii: One knave persuades another
to ambitious thievery, claiming fern-seeds'
miniscule spores
            bestow invisibility.
By sympathetic magic, the science of the day,
plants consign their properties to men:
if fern seed is invisible, so, too,
                        the two of them.

Thus, our thieves, already counting stolen gold,
can scoff at risk, as we in the audience—

who've scoffed at far more deadly schemes
      and lived—
scoff these days at everything.
We've gazed into the sun and now endure
our denouement—a world
          of blur.

Luck

They'd anchored that morning off Malden Island
to witness the first atomic trials. Summoned to formation

in newly-issued masks and safety-suits, they stood around
on deck for what seemed hours, then were ordered

     to attention just before the blast.

Fifty years later, at the bar of his North Sea B&B,
he brags how the lads, sick of the rigmarole and fuss,

coaxed the officers to relent: for subsequent blasts
they'd simply wear their shades and turn their backs,

     they'd be "quite safe."

Quite bored, in fact. Every day they rowed ashore
with an amateur botanist of their number, collecting seeds

of local ferns. Evenings, they caught and ate the fish.
But the cloud, he told me, *was a wonder.*

     Every time, spectacular!

He's the one who said it: *color of rare steak.*
He wants it clear: he's proud to have been present—

the Royal Navy, history, and all—proud these fifty years.
And even now.

Though now, he says, *we know.*

He laughs and claims he's waiting every day
to wake up glowing. Says, the way he sees it,

he's been lucky—missed the war, seen the world,
safe home to tell the story.

Teach Us To Number Our Days

. . . that we may gain a heart of wisdom.
—PSALM 90:12

i. *Via Negativa*

Even now, in desert wastes,
saints are stalking God with terrible intent—

erasing images, attributes, names,
until no likeness to our kind remains.

Only then can they kill him.

> *What saints know: the weight of their failings,*
> *the number of the beast, that the sun will fall*
>
> *and rise again upon their unslaked need*
> *to see God face to face.*

On the far side of the veil, God
is learning to limp, lose his way, count his steps.

He intends to join us.

> *What God knows: our hearts before he formed us*
> *in our mother's womb, the precise articulation*
>
> *of our bones, all that will become of us—*
> *the paint-by-number of our dust.*

If they meet, the saints and their God, it won't be
in anyone's lifetime.

♦

Elsewhere, glacial sheets advance by incremental bits,
trees fall in boreal forests, owls fall upon prey, whales

intone their odes, the wind touches everything once,
and again.

A billion seeds and a star in a galaxy's spiral arm
explode.

ii. The Least of These

Ants are gathering *manna* fallen from the sun—
spiders, desert beetles, ticks. They hunt mid-day

when their predators sleep, scour the narrow ledge
between heat-death and a food chain rife with lizards.

> *What ants know: to forage,*
> *to find their way home.*

God loves the desert's sift and revision, the particled
movement of dunes, the disciplined way his creatures cleave

to the basics: lay pheromone trails, care for their young,
bury their dead, kill, are killed.

He observes all this with the perfect detachment he learned
from his study of scientists.

♦

When the sun burns directly overhead, experiments begin:
techs blot pheromone trails to obscure the scent

of the home nest, then sever one antenna from each ant's head,
consigning her, by these removals, to a landscape of blur.

What scientists know: statistics, meticulous observation,
the keeping of impeccable records.

"Repeatable, repeatable, repeatable,"
they mutter: a mantra.

Call her *Odysseus.*

At the far point of her slog where he's scattered the dead,
a tech lifts Odysseus and clips off her legs at the "knee."

Undeterred, she shoulders a corpse and heads homeward
until, at precisely the half-way point, frantically waving

her one antenna, she halts: lost. You'll say it's the pain
of her wounded limbs pressed again and again

into blistering sands. You'll be wrong.

Now, to the feet of a second Odysseus the tech superglues
a tiny set of pig-hair stilts. Released, she seizes spider flesh,

and, setting off in her seven-league boots, she reaches home
and strides right past—by exactly the 50% predicted.

> *What Odysseus knows astounds the scientists:*
> *how to count her steps.*

iii. In Another Part of the Wilderness

August 1945, Wendover Air Force Base

At a secret base near the Great Salt Flats,
enlisted men assigned to the assembly of the bomb

are missing home. Signs bristling with arrows
record the distance to each boy's hometown.

At night in the barracks, they stare straight up
counting their enlistment down.

Meanwhile, on another part of the base,
B-29 crews toss in dreams, rehearsing their mission.

They've dropped their leaflets on a dozen cities,
promising *prompt and utter destruction*,

urging civilian evacuation. But as for the actual targets,
the boys are not told.

Elsewhere, President Truman prays for the guidance
of the Lord, that we might use our atom bomb

in His ways and for His purposes.

August 2015, Wendover Air Force Base

The floors of the emptied barracks are warped, their roofs
collapsed; no glass is left in the window frames.

Nightly, Wendover frees its ghosts to the foraging winds.
Together the ghosts and the winds scour

a desert still fenced with barbed wire and posted
with warnings: *Danger. Unexploded land mines.*

♦

Over inexpressible stretches of time,
the furnace of the sun burns everything off.

Images, attributes, names.
Pheromone trails. Detachment. Thirst.

Yes, even thirst. Even terrible intent.
On the far side of the veil, God is taking forever.

If we meet, it won't be in anyone's lifetime.

iv. Teach Us To Number

Elsewhere, we grow up, we grow old, we go on
with our counting:

silos, scarecrows, red-winged blackbirds,
cows in the fields that line the two-lane home,

our blessings, the wrongs committed in our name,
loved ones missing from holiday tables,

body bags, refugees, collateral damage,
genocides down to *never again*—

our days our days our days.

Dark Doctrine

Out back in the easement, appetites flourish,
ruthless economies scurry or lurk

(think ambush, think pounce), each creature wise
to its own dual nature: predator / prey.

Progenitor, too—all futures bent to the arc
of probability: slim and nil at opposite endpoints.

Earth's hard to love, a duplicitous place,
where light arrives disguised as bounty,

stays to infest the tender new buds
with impossible urges—to suck the sun's throat

forever. Instead: briefness, death. At first,
it's a hard lesson. Then, just the world.

But lately, dark forces have come to light
in our equations: it seems the bulk of things skulk,

undetected, unlit. Turns out, we're *obscurivores*,
eating the dark and pierced in return by a host

of insurgents we never saw coming.
It's true, nothing's changed in the easement.

We learned to ignore the muffled chewing;
we'll learn to ignore the dark-matter drone

that mars, like static, Enlightenment's sound track.
Consumers by nature, we view this as merely

a parallel feast—of consciousness on error,
each successive worldview devouring the last.

Our mistake was to think it was over,
our knowledge complete. But then,

we're always convinced it's over, as we sink
in a deepening litter of unknown unknowns.

How To Build a Tower To Reach to the Heavens

Gather the chips and discards scattered
on logging roads through old growth forests.

Order a crate of white rhino bones;
grind them to powder.

Walk the shorelines collecting bleached coral.
Add water—not much, tap is fine. Compress.

Of these and the sun, make bricks.

For mortar, Sahara sand is best: pure quartz grains
fallen to Earth when, thousands of years ago

vaporized rock rained down from Mars. (It's true.
Look it up.) Use three parts sand to one part cement.

For extra adhesion, add estuary water.
If not available, sidewalk salt.

High winds can be fearsome; a scoop of lime
reduces fractures. Battlegrounds stock it.

Knead—it won't rise on its own.

Take precautions: Work only at night.
Listen for drones. Avoid the full moon.

Finally, before you begin, consider:
you *will* spend forever.

And your children. And theirs. It will never end.
Please, if there's time, return to the caves.

Ask leave to enter. Cut out your tongues.

Guilt Litany

Have mercy
on the old and ill,
      clothed in what came,
      this day, to hand,
      their buttons misaligned,
      their Velcro'd shoes;
on those awaiting word—
      the hospice call, the cop
      at the door, the ultrasound;
on men and women off their meds
      and on their own,
      the long unsheltered
      asleep in doorways or
      roaming the dark
      pastures of the mind,
      the embittered, the defeated,
      the unloved;
on brutalized children
      of brutalizing times,
      kids cutting themselves
      to watch the blood
      well up, that they might cry
      for something they can see;
on migrant camps,
      the lack of firewood,
      the likelihood
      of rape;
on hope,
      thwarted by concertina wire,
      dogs, surveillance drones;
on fear,
      holding its breath
      in desert darkness
      until our headlights pass;

on those imprisoned
      for misdeeds, missteps,
      mistakenness,
      for justice, vengeance,
      chance.
on the poor we have
      too rarely with us;
and on the useless well-to-do
      who scroll their op-eds,
      sign petitions, write senators
      or litanies,
      willing such things to be
      enough;
on me, on me.

The Divestments
of Autumn

The Divestments of Autumn

We must love life before loving its meaning.
—FYODOR DOSTOEVSKY

i. As above, so below

Late twilight, early autumn,
high distressing winds in the cottonwoods and locusts.
Scores of the dying drift from the branches
to lodge in the understory.
As above, so below.

How did I learn
this discontent? Not from the cottonwoods and locusts,
calm as ever in their autumn losses. Nor from
the Rose of Sharon bearing her crown
of the seasonal dead.

A barred owl dips
and crosses my vision in a ghost-gray hush with death
in its talons, its shadow-wings passing
over the bushes where mute birds
huddle,

smaller than their voices,
smaller than their heartbeats. Earth, ancient alchemist,
tends her transparencies—water, air, fire—
bent on the transfiguration
of light.

Humble down, I tell myself.
Love this.

ii. Twenty-nine bones

It's about the People, who have stopped believing
because the cup of evil has run over.
—DIMITRI SHOSTAKOVICH, SPEAKING OF
HIS *ELEVENTH SYMPHONY,* SUBTITLED *1905*

It happened the year before he was born, but everyone
knew the story, how the Tsar's soldiers dragged

through St. Petersburg's streets
a sled burdened with massacred children.

They had climbed the trees for a glimpse
of the soldiers, their uniforms and guns. Laughing,

the soldiers shot them. The children, too,
laughing, their corpses smiling.

Twenty-nine bones in a human face.
Children. Smiling.

◆

Nineteen-nineteen. *Petrograd* now. A prodigy
starving in a shattered city, his family, too, starving,

Dmitri played nightly for the silent films. His job
asked nothing commensurate with his genius,

only to sight-read a music scored in the huge,
mute faces of light on the screen above him,

faces encoded with a noble suffering—always
for love. Love in the lit bones of the faces,

the theater packed, the audience starving.
Humble down, he told himself.

Love this,
like everybody else.

iii. A language incomprehensible

Chaos instead of Music
—HEADLINE IN *PRAVDA*,
JANUARY 1936

It opened to awe, to ovations, all of Petrograd
lauding his *Lady Macbeth of Minsk.*

Then Stalin himself attended and the show closed.
Had he seen himself in the predatory Lady?

No surprise when the NKVD arrived at Dmitri's door.
No surprise either that, in a heartbeat, the artist recanted.

But how to recant an opera?

"I've begun to speak," he confessed, "in a language
incomprehensible to the People."

Witnesses claimed he was pale, he stuttered,
again and again he adjusted his glasses,

but he bowed to the humbling for the sake
of the uncomprehending People.

And soon it was: Come home, Dmitri,
all is forgiven.
                    Stalin

Absolved, Shostakovich was designated
a Soviet Hero for music exalting the proletariat.

Meanwhile, his fearless string quartets
began filling the dark of a locked desk drawer,

terror in the scoring, death in the strings.
They were never performed.

iv. As above, so below

                             In the glass, my face
with leaves falling through it, dusk's familiar
cellophane self. Out in the darkening yard,
branches and flitting birds
tangle themselves

                          in my reflection,
complicating my vision. By swift
shifts of focus, I cast and erase
my face from the glass,
peeling the tissues

                          from a wound
forever on the verge of healing.
Soon, I'll abandon this game,
snap the light, and
disperse.

                         ◆

                         Seek His face,
the Psalmist tells us. Late autumn's face is lean
as an oboe—bony brow, haggard gaze.
If the face of God were to peel
from this sky

                         and peer down upon us
in our own image, it might be something
like this—as if from an unsuspected
dimension curled inside
an eternal caesura,

                         we discerned the voice
of a solo viola rising from nowhere's ruins
bearing unbearable sweetness. Instead:

this expanding drone
suggesting

                      a cosmic confession,
a recantation so intimate, so dire,
it cannot be acknowledged:
God's apology (too late)
for Time.

               Seek His face.
But if God were to bend his brooding countenance
even once above our dispirited planet
and linger, perfectly constant,
perfectly remote,

                  would we notice?
Would we sense a stirring of the hairs at our nape?
Taste a sweetness? A chlorophyll-ing? Feel
a leafiness or the hint of a heightened
affinity for light?

I find it unlikely.

v. Humble down. Love this.

Full dark now. Walking my neighborhood in the chill
of winter's first cut, my eyes are drawn to a woman's face

sliced by rectangular panes of glass—a mosaic above a sink
where an aloe plant spikes from one pane to another.

Eyes lifted from her work, she gazes out over her lawn,
hands immersed in filmy water, wrists broken at the waterline.

Or so I imagine.

From her place in the light, she won't see me pass.
She's watching the dark mask of her face,

while time stirs its ever-transfiguring flames,
and earth turns us into our dispersal.

vi. Atonement

Shame is the feeling that saves mankind.
—ANDREI TARKOVSKY
SPEAKING OF SHOSTOKOVICH

I've set my CD on continual replay. Each time it begins—
the great *dies irae* of the *Tenth* with its *ostinato* droning beneath

his elaborate scorings—it lifts the flesh of my forearms
with its secret, Cyrillic encrypting of his name.

     D E-flat C B.   *D E-flat C B.*

Who was it who first deciphered the code—the broken
elegist's cry rising ghostly from the orchestra's depths

to speak his name and dissolve?
Even de-coded and long after everyone's death,

it remains an incomprehensible presence.
A plea for forgiveness? A brutal re-wounding?

An act of feeble defiance? Again tonight, I try to summon
some measure of healing from history's silent film,

but no coded message breaks free to reveal a meaning
lodged in the brittle, ongoing, black-and-white flicker.

     Only complicity.

Who first understood the divestments of autumn,
recognized chlorophyll's crazed after-burn as thirst?

Who first heard this lushest of all Earth's scores—
briefness, brittleness, ghost—as grief?

     How to recant an age?

Autumn: a gorgeous sear of the air, but always
beneath the crescendo of beauty,

the drone of atonement.

How It Is We Have Come to This

How It Is We Have Come to This

We will not die in the world we were born to.
        Already, so much has been lost.
How it came to be lost will be told to prove
        our unworthiness. Even now, we title
our chronicles: *How It Is We Have Come to This*.

        They tell of how, on our heedless watch,
the waters rose or hordes swept through;
        how plague came followed by
drought or drought came followed by plague.
        Worse, how once, in the time

of our testing, a relic was left in our keeping.
        A slice of noontime darkness?
Splinters of a life-line crushed at the foot
        of a cross? A halo bone unearthed
in a tomb? It's all a bit vague, but

        the relic was lost. In the wake
of our failing we've clung to what's left:
        a consoling dark we cup
in our folded hands—not enough
        to keep our children from leaving.

They're sailing west now, seeking Eden.
        We know what that search
will come to: nothing. It's hard here
        without them. But lately, travelers
have come to our shores with tales

        of heroes whose names are familiar,
tales of great trials, great triumphs, great
        loves, happy endings. These, too,
are familiar. Worse, they ring true: each one
        contains the world we will die in.

Turning and Turning

AFTER W.B. YEATS'S "THE SECOND COMING"

To keep their accustomed distance from the sun,
      the falcons circle higher now,
            and maybe in a world like ours, scored
with crosshairs, tripwires, sightlines,
      it's wise to feign remove, but this—
            this is something more.

Dwarfed already in the widening heavens, the sun
      backs further off—toward shun. Clouds race west,
            glad to shake our dust from their hems.
Below, we circle our rooms, window to window.
      Something is missing: a beat, a link.
            Were there signs? Were we watching?

Glaciers escape into oceans, their disguise
      impeccable. Floods brazen through plains
            uprooting crops, bio-tech corridors,
the gated enclaves of the well-to-do. Curls
      spiral down too soon from the crowns
            of corkscrew willows, carving

narrow keyholes for a pitiless sky to leer through:
      something has us in its sights. It seems
            we belong to a far-sighted god
who has seen us at last for the creatures we are,
      puny at heart, though puffed with huff
            and umbrage: prodigal children.

Why didn't we listen:
      A cold homecoming you'll have of it.
        Dim of vision, you'll huddle

in hazed cities, short of breath and shivering,
      your souls powdered and needled,
            your sleep dismantled.

Something like that. Something
            about beasts. About circling birds
                  of prey. Deserts. Darkness.
Nothing about repentance.
            No second chances. No mention
            of saviors.

The Woman Taken in Adultery

Years of men's voices speaking of need, speaking
of cost. Or not speaking at all, just reaching, taking.

Years of hurried meetings where coins change hands—
and nothing else changes.

Centuries of this before stones drop from fists,
something gets written in dust, and a voice says

Woman—, says *Go*—. After which: silence.

The parable ends the same for us now,
no matter what words were written in that dust,

or written in her heart, or later on her grave,
or written, mis-written, on a cross.

And we, too, must go. But where? And what
will become of us now?

To be fair, he was not told, either.

Nothing changes in this world. We go our way
leaving only our dust, from which,

if any message lifts, it dissolves, undelivered.
It's all illegible anyway, every transaction.

Needs unmet. Costs uncounted.
Nothing can shift the stone

from this story's ellipsis.

Mating with Angels

We weren't much more than kids
        when we first took up with angels—

double-yoked creatures of flesh and light,
        so wicked-bright it hurt to look.

        We mated in the dark.

Every coupling tore us to the core and left us
        no less ravenous, no less alone.

We should have guessed from the distances
        they kept. Instead, we let them pledge

        eternal love. So much for promises.

In truth, we're glad they're gone; they never
        liked us much. When the initial glow

wore off, we steeled ourselves to view them
        in full sun—we saw right through them.

        It took us far too long.

Now we face the aftermath: toxicities simmer
        in our children's blood. No wings yet,

but they whisper together, disputing the source
        of their fledgling glory, their lack of appetite,

        their ardent wish to soar.

This year they all wear white on white exclusively,
        maintain in their clubs a rigid hierarchy.

And all of them are musical. What are the odds?
How, they demand, could *they* have come

from *us?* It's time we confessed.

Protective measures will need to be taken. Soon.
It's a hard world for the winged. Hard, too,

to ask them to resist the tumultuous urges
of their blood—that all-consuming need

to love, lay waste, flee the scene.

One day they'll swab their cheeks or send off
their spit for DNA analysis. On that day,

nothing we say will matter in the least: they'll
test their wings, and for our sins,

we will be blessed to death. Or doomed.

If a Tree Falls in a Forest
and No One

Would it have mattered if, as children, we'd been taught
        to attend to the vanishing? If we'd practiced to hear

the migrating songbirds churring above us each fall
        or the waning buzz of insect wings in the meadow

as summer lifted away? If we'd risen at dawn to witness
        the synchronized hatch of a thousand mayflies,

or trained our ears to catch the squeals of bats
        in the evening fields or an elephant's

low-pitched mourning for one of its own? What if
        we'd tuned our hearing to sift the fine strains

of silence when silence still augured nothing
        more dire than a shift of season?

I read this week that a billion songbirds die each year
        in the U.S. alone, head-butting a hard glass sky

in a rush to drive off their own reflections. A billion.
        How vast a caesura. But not once have I noticed

the hush I wake to on New Year's morning,
        another year over and a billion birds missing.

If a single tree fell—to lightning or ice-storm, to blight,
        to flame, or to trucks come to clear-cut the lots

for the new subdivisions—would anyone hear it?
        Would life be different if we'd learned as kids

to gauge the pitch of the wind-hum or hear songs
        of loss in the evening rain? How long have I

been hard enough of heart to accept the slam
        of a bird smashing headlong against the glass

of my sunroom? Or so hard of hearing I miss
        the crash of a forest falling?

Special Pleading

If each of us were to plead for one endangered species . . .

I'd plead for emerald dragonflies: skin shimmering
in arsenic green, isinglass wings, eyes
as transfixing as slaughter.
                            Three hundred million
years ago, this dragonfly's precursors steered
a three-foot wingspan through Pangea's swamps,
wielding a predatory grace.
                            Diminished now,
they weave their specialized weaponry through
a smoke of mosquitos, carving out hollows
in their wake.
                            If you love them,
you have to love them fast—or start early,
tromping the shores of shallow ponds to praise
their wingless humps
                            afloat in scum.
By the time they lift from the waters,
four years will have passed in your own
endangered life.
                            But it's time well spent.
Your reward will be two glorious months
of watching them scatter the light as they
hover and dart,
                            mate and hunt
in ferocious splendor. Such is the fleeting use
our profligate Earth makes of beauty. But now,
their days as a species
                            are numbered,
a slide it's unlikely my prayers can stop.
Even so, it's these dragonflies I'd plead for
in the hope that a member
                            of whatever species

next rules earth might happen upon
a single, exquisite, tissue-glass wing
lodged in the grasses.

Sometimes to Our Sorrow

Stalking the base of a cinderblock wall,
a stub-tailed cat pours itself forward
                and re-compacts,

its step menace-slow and light as a lick.
I would not want to be small prey
                in these fields.

In the middle distance, sun shafts loll
on buckling roofs and ruffle the fur
                of shed-boards,

a scene of laudable ruin. Some days,
it strikes me as good to be weathered.
                Chipped. Un-repainted.

I've grown tired of sweetness. I favor salt—
less indulgent, more honest.
                Chemically, salt is a pact

of poisons: sodium/chlorine. We sow it
to our sorrow. But then, I savor sorrow, too:
                it tastes of truth.

It's autumn now. Seeds of black walnut trees
lie scattered in tough green husks
                on the lawns,

tossed ripe onto toxic ground at the foot
of the parent tree, where they'll rot
                or be eaten.

Only a few—carried off and buried
by squirrels, frozen, forgotten—will gain
                from the deep cold

the right to a future. It's an ugly bargain:
one generation blights the earth; the next
                    lights out for the territories.

I know I've taken safety for granted, as if
it were earned. Still, as my life nears its end,
                    it's enough

to sit in the sun admiring the stalk
of a molten cat—a practiced combatant,
                    its weapons honed.

By contrast, my own kind has mastered
the strike-from-afar—a meld of accuracy
                    and denial that lets us

live with ourselves. And yes, times change.
Sometimes to our sorrow. I would not want
                    to be a terrorist in this world.

Or a child.

O Holy Night

In the easement,
bare trees daven apathetically
under a skull-cap sky.
                    Oh, Child,
are you sure? This world?
This bleak winter?
These unconscionable times?

The last of the day's feeble sun
steeps the holly,
staining its berries a deep
                    crimson
as bright and slick
as a seasoned trickster, then
slips off the edge of the earth,

leaving to us this night,
first among too many nights
we've marked
                    and mean,
every year, to find holy.
It's getting old, this act.
Or maybe it's me. Lately,

I'm all lapse and misstep.
And yet, love's tiny fist seeks out
my heart with the old entreaty,
                    and yearly
I somehow let in love enough
to try again: to call our people
decent, our planet worthy.

Vinegar

If it's true, as they say, that our neurons can't tell
a memory of rain from a coming-down storm
or a grizzly on film from an actual beast;
if the word *ice-cream* tastes as sweet to our neurons
as real dessert, shouldn't life be a piece of cake?

> *Envision world peace.*
> *Meditate to perfect your tennis serve.*
> *Take both parts in the dialogue of prayer.*

But what kind of fool would settle for love's
neuronal shadow on the cranium wall,
a *postcard* of Paris, a *mirage* in the desert?
Even Jesus asked for his water drawn cold from a well,
and when, at the end, thirst raged on that hill,
a sponge of vinegar tasted, I'm sure,
exactly like vinegar.

Try it: envision yourself a thief.
You've known all your life
it's a world of harm owned entirely by others.
Your death has been decreed; this day, your last.
You know all this. But still, you speak:

> *Remember me, Lord.*

Now, close your eyes and imagine him
imagining you (there are worse definitions
of love) this day in his kingdom, healed, made whole.
The next thing you know, you're alive and well,
swinging axon branches inside the skull
of a dying god.

Except, just now, he's a dying man,
his mind, like yours, a kingdom lit by neurons

leaping a trillion synaptic abysses toward . . .
what?
Nothingness? Paradise?

And yes, it's still *that* leap of faith.

The Late
Accommodations

The Late Accommodations

The human eye can discern 500 shades of gray.

Five hundred grays, most of them nameless,
      and maybe that's best. Take Lear
on the heath, stripped to the battering cold.
      Though mad, he saw human wretchedness
clearly, called it by name: *The thing itself,*
      unaccommodated man, a poor,
bare, forked animal. Yes. Us.

It's dusk. I've been driving all afternoon
      down one of those thin blue highways
veining my state, alone and buffeted by loss.
      The horse appears on a rise where shadows
lean over a moon-gray pasture—owl-gray,
      pearl-gray, dapple-gray. When my list
runs out, I'll be back in the road-hum, stuck
      with my heartbeat and sorrows. Instead,

I pull to the shoulder to watch the mare,
      her muzzle moving through gauzy grasses,
an unhurried scythe cropping toward me.
      A lopsided moon casts shivers of light
down over her, glinting her eyes and draping
      her flesh in a silver-gray mantle.
Cerecloth. Shakespeare invented the word.
      A soothing balm of syllables: *cerements.*

As her shape loses definition—slate gray,
      shadow-gray, ghost—I hear Lear's
shattered voice (*Look there, look there!*)
      as he struggles to deny what no one can.
And these are life's late accommodations:
      consenting to ease a shape we love—

and even, in time, our poor, bare, forked selves—
    toward erasure, and on, into a vast,
accommodating field of anonymous shades.

This Is the Hour

Hour when jays patrolling the pine forest
        segue into their quick evening calls.

Hour of spring peepers, newly emerged
        from a winter remission under the leaf litter.

Hour of the cats' reappearance, sloping in
        from the barn or stepping imperiously

down from the study. Hour of the porch swing
        vacantly stirring. Time to be heating

last evening's chowder, setting it to simmer.
        Supper hour. Hour when the neighbor's dog

in its third incarnation sounds the alarm—some
        harmless stranger passing on the walk.

Headstones in the plot at the base of the slope
        hold the light of a lowering sun,

the granite flashing a silver blank. No words
        disturb the quiet. Maybe he hums a bit

over the stove or murmurs a word
        to one of the cats, nothing much.

It seems to have changed the planes of his face,
        keeping his voice so still for so long.

His eyes rest unfocused on a piece of the dusk
        where the newest stone's shadow

blends with the trees—*her* trees, *her* stone.
This is the hour he feels most acutely

the slow roll of Earth that carries them on, the hour
when, sometimes, he speaks her name.

Woman, Why Are You Weeping

Easter morning. Luminous clouds clot the sky, a reminder
    that now is now, and later is another story.

PeterPeterPeter, chides a titmouse on the fence, but Peter,
    I'm sure, feels bad enough already. Saturday

must have been dreadful. Sunday, when news arrived
    from the garden—*empty, angels*—it's said that,

alongside beloved John, Peter tore headlong to the tomb.
    Which is odd. How could *empty* mean anything good?

Plots, grave robbers, wild beasts. Was he that desperate
    to be forgiven? I long, like Peter, for miracles

but, of late, *Hallelujahs* are hard to come by. The sky here
    is nearly black: darkness at noon. Weighted clouds,

the color of stones—slate, shale, flint. Or the grim shade
    a cotton ball turns when it's dipped in astringent—

shade of the infamous sponge of vinegar. What made God think
    a mortal life might be the slightest bit bearable?

My mother is in hospice now. I've watched her dementia
    worsen, a diminishment stretched over years.

Each morning, she wakes whole and young, tries to rise
    and begins to cry, asking whoever is holding her hand,

"Where is John? Where is John?" Is *this* life worth living?
    Today is Easter. She woke, as always, bewildered,

begging this stranger, her daughter, to tell her the truth:
    how she came to be lying in this strange room.

Is she sick? Dying? What's wrong that she doesn't remember her name? And please, please, where is John?

Rain Song Refrain

Rain
at the glass,
cutting April's dusk with quick
random wires, sheeting
from eaves back-lit by porch lights,
soaking the bricks with a stain
as enduring as lichen on stone.

Rain
on a third day,
a fourth, a fifth, until we stop asking,
Will it ever stop? No. It goes on
through the night of his death—
rain borne downriver on a hearse
of thunder, rain draped in black.

Rain
in the aftermath,
drenching the parking lot, lashing
the stained glass, slashing ornamentals.
Unseasonable rain, edging into ice
on the path to his gravesite, battering
the canopy, softening the turned earth.

Rain
in the hush tonight,
falling on stone, falling on cedars
whose limbs release odors
unchanged from the day when the first
human grief entered time, and to rain
was assigned the music of

endlessness.

Until There Are Roses

Cross-legged on the floor of the dark
guest closet, I breathed in the scent
of woolen coats, rubber boots, and a cold
        so immaculate it hurt.
Winds rose to lash the leaded-glass window,
the weatherproofing moaned. Outside
the closed door, my sister had died.
        Our histories unroll
apportioned into seasons, each of mine
marked by a burial I missed: too young,
too hard, too far.
        The next death is coming.
I'll have no say, but I hope it's not snarled
in difficult travels, flights delayed, icy roads.
The tasks of this passing will be mine.
        My mother died
on Mother's Day the year I was nine.
From my high bedroom window, on the morning
of the service, I watched my grandmother
        gathering roses
below in my mother's garden—a half-filled
basket, slim, silver shears. It all seemed so slow:
I watched her sink to her knees and fold.
        My brother died
in April in a faraway city, surrounded
by friends I didn't know. We sang him
out of the world with verses
        I memorized that night
in his long last hours. When I didn't return
for his service, I'm told, his friends allowed me
a loving reason.
        Ice storms predicted.
I'm sitting in the dark tonight confessing to only
my heart how poorly I've lived in death's
aftermath. Another death is coming. I pray,

not yet. Maybe after
the holidays? But not in the first frozen months
of the year, limbs bare, winds howling. Maybe
in spring? I can bear it in spring. Maybe wait,
                    until there are roses?

History

Each summer as evenings shortened, the sheen
on our glacial lake deepened to pewter

and something nameless opened in me
like a time-lapse wounding. Out on the porch,

three generations aligned their breathing
to the synchronized arcs of four wicker rockers.

Griefs were alluded to there in low tones, voices
lifting a long-ago sorrow and letting it sink again

into silence. I was a child, I'd only half-listen,
drifting in and out of their lives and my own.

Over the years, new losses accrued in our family
like sheet ice thickening out on the lake.

We were summer people, long gone by first snow,
but according to north woods legend there came

a night deep in winter when wolves would appear
crossing the ice in a ghostly light, as if on tiptoe—

a silent, unlikely procession of lives
the locals claimed had always lived in those woods.

On the far shore, under the northern lights,
they'd take up their burden of keening. A night

of unearthly beauty. Or, so we were told.
Who can say in the Northwoods what's true?

Our elders are gone now, the rest of us scattered.
In dreams sometimes I hear those vanished voices

and listen hard for the missing bits of our story,
but too many winters have passed since their passing.

Was there a time when wolves moved soundlessly
through the forest, when our shallow lake

ran cold and deep and lumber trucks rumbled
out on the highway, the mines still thriving?

Some things are beyond retrieval, but somehow
those earlier lives of hurt and endurance passed

into mine and became mine to guard, until
one day I understood I would have to love them.

Single Things

Above a tangled end-of-season garden, a lone crow
        eyes me from a shed's collapsing roof.

Below, on its doorstep, the merest scrim of sun.
        Earlier, out on Hwy M, in an otherwise empty

meadow, a horse stood under a bleached-out sky,
        unmoving, with only a spindly windbreak

to keep him from the sweep of miles. It's not the winds
        or the solitude. It's the impossibility of knowing

how far the fields stretch beyond you. Or the days.

Down by the tracks, I meet a man walking a bike.
        We smile and nod. Soon, November's torrents

will hustle us both indoors and pin these dead leaves
        to the lawns. At an intersection of trails,

I rest on a bench, half-hidden, only big enough for one.
        Everywhere, guarded solitudes. Even the grasses,

bowed by horizontal winds, are separate creatures
        subject to the one force. A prairie takes on

a different life in winter. By winter, I'll be gone.

Heading back, I ponder the odd grain of identity:
        fingerprint whirls, swirls of lichen

down the length of a trunk, the synchronous turn
        of turbines on wind farms spread over the plains.

Cities. Towns. The roads between. Single things
        embedded in a landscape of collective nouns.

Are we all in this together? I remember the hum
        of Sunday prayers, a unison as seamless

as the garment they say Jesus wore to the cross.
        And the rosary beads in the elders' fingers

counting the decades toward the understood ending.

These days, I watch my father's hands counting
        his meds. No act I can think of is more alone.

In late sun, shallow ponds transmute to tarnished beads.
        Trail markers stand in their own shadows

like stations of the cross. I make my way from one
        to the next tallying singularities: an attempt

to keep something nameless nonetheless whole.

'Rivers Wanted

Here's a fact:

Every time you strike *B-flat*—
oboe, cello, flute, whatever—

alligators bellow in flat-out joy.
That's how they phrased it: *flat-out joy*.

Here's another: Deep in the heart
of the Perseus cluster, a black hole

transmits a cosmic Om—
B-flat again.

Okay, it's fifty-seven octaves
below middle-C.

And true, it pulses only once
in each ten million years.

And yes, to hear it you'd need
an ear the size of a galaxy,

not to mention a length of life
no gator has yet achieved.

But still.

But still, there are days I can't
shake this sadness.

The world's unjust, unkind, undone.
The news gets only worse.

Or outright weird. In a recent study,
musicians were asked simply

to breathe and, when ready, to sing
one note, whatever came.

North Americans sang *B-flat.*
Europeans, *G-sharp.* No exceptions.

Of course, there's a logical
explanation: electrical currents.

America runs on sixty cycles
per second; in Europe, it's fifty.

B-flat; G-sharp.
We are hooked up and hummed to,

thrummed through from birth.
Or maybe something in our universe

loves us.

Take today, for example.
Ahead on the highway,

there's a semi- bearing the usual ad
'RIVERS WANTED.

One missing letter and I'm struck
with lust—the muscled rush

of currents, crushing desire,
breathlessness—the trundling world,

all eighteen wheels, singing in pure
B-flat. And yes,

I'm still stuck in rush hour traffic
on a highway lined with slush,

behind a truck I can't see past. But
something in the universe loves me,

is pulsing my personal frequency.
So what, if life's a cosmic code

I mostly can't break? So what,
if maybe it's me who's broken?

Why not try it, a flat-out bellow?
What can I lose?

Only my heart—again. As if
it were spring.

As if I were young.

How To Disappear

. . . like a plain, simple thing.
—HANS CHRISTIAN ANDERSEN
THE NIGHTINGALE

     Keep still so long
time comes to rest
like dust
on your shoulders.
Then, thin yourself
till it lifts from your skin
like a cloud of gnats
in a gold cast of sun.
Now,
thin further.
     Or,
if you'd rather,
linger a while, clothed
in a world-colored substance
that can't be told
from the whole.
Which of you, then—
figure or ground—
is ghost?
     It's one of the long arts.
Give it time.
Let all the sweet grief
at your passing pass,
until—de-moted
from every eye that filled
even once with your face—
you are free to be off
at light-speed.
Exceed yourself.
     If you feel at first
the urge to return,

to assure yourself
of your absence,
that's fine. Re-cohere
from your memory of flesh
a provisional presence.
Perch on a limb
out of sight. Sing.
   Sing
your diminishment.
Sing like an echo returned
from the shores
of an old fairy tale. Sing,
like a plain, simple thing.
   No love
need be revisited now;
no sin remains
to be undone.
Release your name,
your past, your dust.
Only now it begins—
the *after,* the *life.*

Notes

"The Laws of Perspective": The epigraph is taken from John Berger's *The Sense of Sight* (Vintage International, 1993).

"In the Cave": The quotation in the epigraph is taken from Peter Singer's *Animal Liberation* (Harper Collins, 1975).

"The Divestments of Autumn": Material concerning the life of Dimitri Shostakovich, including the direct quotation in part iii., is taken from Stephen Jackson's 1997 book, *Dimitri Shostakovich: An Essential Guide to His Life and Works* (Pavilion Books).

"This Is the Hour" is in memory of my dear friend Monty Leitch.

"Woman, Why Are You Weeping" is in memory of my father, John Herweg, and my stepmother, Dorothy Glahn Herweg.

"Rain Song Refrain" is in memory of my brother, Jim Herweg.

"Until There Are Roses" is in memory of my sister Judy, my brother Jim, and my mother, Janet Scovill Herweg.

Acknowledgments

Acknowledgment and thanks to the editors of the following publications in which the poems listed below, some in slightly different form, first appeared.

The American Literary Review	"The Laws of Perspective"
Beloit Poetry Journal	"The Divestments of Autumn"
Boulevard	"Precious Oils"
Canary	"Tremolo"
Chariton Review	"'Rivers Wanted"
Conclave	"The Woman Taken in Adultery"
The Cresset	"How To Build a Tower To Reach to the Heavens"
Cumberland River Review	"History," "How To Disappear," & "Single Things"
December	"Lack"
Flyway	"Toxic Nocturne"
Gargoyle	"Unjust"
The Gettysburg Review	"Dark Doctrine," "In the Cave," & "The Lost Blue of Chartres"
The Hudson Review	"We Walk Invisible"
I-70 Review	"Rain Song Refrain," "This Is the Hour," & "Turning and Turning"
Image	"Canticle of Want"
Innisfree	"Early Onset with Quicksand and Pythons"

Lullwater Review	"Special Pleading"
One	"Tenebrae"
Poems for Ephesians	"O Holy Night"
Poet Lore	"Mating with Angels"
Prairie Schooner	"Teach Us To Number Our Days," & "Until There Are Roses"
Relief	"Sometimes to Our Sorrow" & "Vinegar"
River Styx	"First Sighting of the Great Salt Flats"
Sisyphus	"Guilt Litany" & "If a Tree Falls in a Forest and No One"
Sou'wester	"Woman, Why Are You Weeping"
The Sow's Ear Poetry Review	"The Angel of Absolute Zero"
Terrene	"Psalm of the Luna Moth"
Tampa Review	"How It Is We Have Come to This"
Water-Stone Review	"The Late Accommodations"

"The Divestments of Autumn" was awarded the 2016 Chad Walsh Poetry Prize from the *Beloit Poetry Journal*.

"The Laws of Perspective" was reprinted in *The Ekphrastic Review*.

"Special Pleading" was reprinted in *Canary*.

"The Lost Blue of Chartres," "How To Disappear," & Special Pleading" were reprinted in *I-70 Review*.

Additional Thanks

I AM DEEPLY GRATEFUL to Bavarian sculptor Alfred Böschl (1949–2020) for providing the cover artwork for *The Angel of Absolute Zero*. Awarded numerous honors for his public sculptures, his many works of sacred art, and his decades of dedication to the Bavarian art community, Böschl was the 2001 recipient of the prestigious *Verleihung des Bundeserdienstkreuzes* (Order of Merit for the Federal Republic of Germany).

Immense gratitude to Barbara Crooker, Jane O. Wayne, and Allison Funk, who read and commented on earlier versions of many of these poems. Their own fine poetry has inspired me, their skilled editing suggestions have made these poems stronger, and their friendship has meant the world to me.

I am indebted to the Virginia Center for the Creative Arts for fellowships that provided me with time, studio space, inspiring surroundings, and the comradeship of gifted writers and artists as I worked on the poems in this volume.

To series editor, Don Martin, who brought thoughtful editing advise and a gimlet eye to the preparation of the manuscript, I am more than grateful. Thanks, too, to those at Cascade Books for their expertise and professionalism.

And thank you again and always, Dan. You are my absolute angel.

The Poiema Poetry Series

COLLECTIONS IN THIS SERIES INCLUDE:

Six Sundays Toward a Seventh by Sydney Lea
Epitaphs for the Journey by Paul Mariani
Within This Tree of Bones by Robert Siegel
Particular Scandals by Julie L. Moore
Gold by Barbara Crooker
A Word In My Mouth by Robert Cording
Say This Prayer into the Past by Paul Willis
Scape by Luci Shaw
Conspiracy of Light by D.S. Martin
Second Sky by Tania Runyan
Remembering Jesus by John Leax
What Cannot Be Fixed by Jill Pelaez Baumgaertner
Still Working It Out by Brad Davis
The Hatching of the Heart by Margo Swiss
Collage of Seoul by Jae Newman
Twisted Shapes of Light by William Jolliff
These Intricacies by David Harrity
Where the Sky Opens by Laurie Klein
True, False, None of the Above by Marjorie Maddox
The Turning Aside anthology edited by D.S. Martin
Falter by Marjorie Stelmach
Phases by Mischa Willett
Second Bloom by Anya Krugovoy Silver
Adam, Eve, & the Riders of the Apocalypse anthology edited by D.S. Martin
Your Twenty-First Century Prayer Life by Nathaniel Lee Hansen
Habitation of Wonder by Abigail Carroll

Ampersand by D.S. Martin
Full Worm Moon by Julie L. Moore
Ash & Embers by James A. Zoller
The Book of Kells by Barbara Crooker
Reaching Forever by Philip C. Kolin
The Book of Bearings by Diane Glancy
In a Strange Land anthology edited by D.S. Martin
What I Have I Offer With Two Hands by Jacob Stratman
Slender Warble by Susan Cowger
Madonna, Complex by Jen Stewart Fueston
No Reason by Jack Stewart
Abundance by Andrew Lansdown
Angelicus by D.S. Martin
Trespassing on the Mount of Olives by Brad Davis